LADYBUGS

INSECTS DISCOVERY LIBRARY

Jason Cooper

Rourke Publishing LLC
Vero Beach, Florida 32964

www.rourkepublishing.com

PHOTO CREDITS: Cover, p. 4, 10, 11 © James H. Carmichael; title page, p. 16, 17, 18, 20, 21 © Joyce Gross; p. 8, 13 © James P. Rowan; p. 9 © Alex Wild; p. 22 © Lynn M. Stone

Title page: A ladybug looks for aphids on a leaf.

Library of Congress Cataloging-in-Publication Data

Cooper, Jason, 1942-
 Ladybugs / Jason Cooper.
      p. cm. -- (Insects discovery library)
 Includes bibliographical references and index.
 ISBN 1-59515-428-0 (hardcover)
 1. Ladybugs--Juvenile literature. I. Title.
 QL596.C65C66 2006
 595.76'9--dc22
                                    2005010972

Printed in the USA

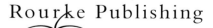
Rourke Publishing

www.rourkepublishing.com – sales@rourkepublishing.com
Post Office Box 3328, Vero Beach, FL 32964
1-800-394-7055

TABLE OF CONTENTS

Ladybugs   5
Ladybug Food   11
Being a Ladybug   14
Young Ladybugs   19
Glossary   23
Index   24
Further Reading/Websites to Visit   24

Ladybugs

Ladybugs are a kind of beetle. Beetles make up a huge family of **insects**.

Beetles have a pair of hard front wings. They fold over their two back wings when they are not flying.

A ladybug perches on a flower.

About 150 kinds of ladybugs live in the United States. Most are orange or yellow with black spots.

A ladybug is shaped like a very small, shiny dome. Several little ladybugs could stand on one dime.

Most ladybugs have black spots.

A ladybug has six legs. It has two pair of wings. It has two **antennas** on its head.

Ladybugs live in woodlands. They live in meadows. They live in gardens. Sometimes they even crawl into houses!

This ladybug shows its antennas.

Ladybug Food

We are not afraid of ladybugs. But insects called **aphids** should be.

Ladybugs gobble up aphids like popcorn! In its short lifetime one ladybug can eat 5,000 aphids.

A ladybug eats an aphid.

11

Ladybugs also eat scale insects.

Most big animals do not like to eat ladybugs. Ladybugs have a bad taste.

Did You Know?
Ladybugs eat the insects that eat the farmers' crops.

This ladybug is eating an insect.

Being a Ladybug

Ladybugs may fly a short distance. More often, they just pull in their legs and antennas.

A ladybug may choose to "hide" instead of fly.

Ladybugs sometimes live together in the fall. As many as 40 million ladybugs may be in the same place.

Some ladybugs sleep winter away. This is called **hibernation**.

A ladybug stretches its two hind wings.

Ladybugs gather in the fall.

Young Ladybugs

During her lifetime a ladybug may lay 300 eggs. The eggs hatch after 3 to 5 days. The baby is a tiny crawling insect. This stage of ladybug life is called the **larva**.

A ladybug larva looks little like an adult.

Ladybug larva eat aphids for two or three weeks. Each larva then changes into a **pupa**.
 A ladybug spends about 7 to 10 days as a pupa.

A ladybug stands on its pupa skin.

An adult ladybug wriggles out of its pupa skin.

GLOSSARY

antennas (an TEN uhz) — thread-like objects on an insect's head; they act as "feelers" and help an insect smell and hear

aphids (AY fidz) — tiny insects that eat plants

hibernation (HY bur NAY shun) — a long winter sleep

insects (IN SEKTZ) — small, boneless animals with six legs

larva (LAR vuh) — a stage of an insect's life before it becomes an adult

pupa (PYU puh) — the quiet, final stage of life for some insects before they become adults

A harlequin beetle is one of the ladybug's cousins.

INDEX

antennas   9, 14

aphids   11, 20

beetle   5

eggs   19

hibernation   17

insects   5

larva   19

legs   9, 14

pupa   20

wings   5, 9

Further Reading

Godkin, Celia. *What about Ladybugs?* Sierra Club, 1998
Schwartz, David M. *Ladybug*. Gareth Stevens, 2001

Websites to Visit

http://www.fcps.k12.va.us/StratfordLandingES/Ecology/mpages/
     convergent_ladybug_beetle.html
http://www.enchantedlearning.com/subjects/insects/Ladybug.shtml

About the Author

Jason Cooper has written many children's books for Rourke Publishing about a variety of topics. Cooper travels widely to gather information for his books.